Louis Sullivan

AND THE CHICAGO SCHOOL

LOUIS SULLIVAN

AND THE CHICAGO SCHOOL

Nancy Frazier

KNICKERBOCKER
PRESS

Published by Knickerbocker Press
276 Fifth Avenue
New York, New York 10001

Produced by Brompton Books Corp.
15 Sherwood Place
Greenwich, Connecticut 06830

ISBN 1-57715-085-6

Printed in China
Printed in 1999

ACKNOWLEDGMENTS
The publisher would like to thank the following people who helped in
the preparation of this book: Ron Callow, Design 23, who designed it;
Kathy Schneider, who did the picture research; Cynthia Klein, who
prepared the index; and John Kirk, who edited the text.

Page 1: Louis H. Sullivan.

Page 2: The ornamented façade
of Sullivan's 1897 Bayard
Building in New York City.

These pages: A portion of the
façade of Sullivan's Guaranty
(Prudential) Building in
Buffalo, NY, built in 1894-95.

Contents

Introduction

It was nine o'clock on Sunday night, October 8, 1871, when Mrs. Patrick O'Leary's cow kicked over an oil lamp and ignited the fire that destroyed Chicago.

While flames spread from O'Leary's barn on the west side of the city to over 2000 acres, people went mad. Some, stunned or crazed, wandered the streets aimlessly, while elsewhere rampaging hoodlums set sofas and bedding afire and looted abandoned houses. On the outskirts of this chaos a group of wealthy industrialists and merchants were relaxing in a mansion they had leased for their newly formed Chicago Club. When news of the fire came they dispersed, but the next day several members who had been burned out of their homes or offices reconvened at the club for breakfast, only to be routed again when the club house itself finally caught on fire. Toting cigars, whisky and a red satin sofa from the sitting room, they moved on to finish breakfast at the lake front.

By Tuesday morning, when rain began to fall, the raging fire seemed under control and the damage could be assessed: 1500 human victims, 17,450 buildings reduced to rubble, 340,000 people homeless.

Chicago's Great Fire is now recalled as a near-legendary disaster, but in strictly architectural terms it was something of a purgative, clearing much prime real estate for redevelopment. In the wake of the Civil War the city had begun to boom as the meat packing and trading center of the country. But the result had been row upon row of wooden tenements, 56 miles of wooden block pavements and 561 miles of wooden sidewalks. Now Chicago's indomitable entrepreneurs hardly missed a beat. Out of the ashes quickly rose the new city that became America's premier architectural showplace. The financial moguls – Field, McCormick, Leiter, Pullman and Peck, for instance – became patrons to the most renowned architects of the day. From out of town they hired Henry Hobson Richardson, Richard Morris Hunt and the firm of McKim, Mead and White, while from the best Chicago firms they hired Henry Ives Cobb, William Le Baron Jenney and the partnerships of Holabird and Roche, Burnham and Root, as well as Dankmar Adler and his young associate, Louis H. Sullivan. And from their drafting tables came a revolution in civic architecture.

As the city reshaped itself, one of its most interesting and controversial of the new designers, Louis H. Sullivan, emerged as the central figure in what would be come to be called the Chicago School of Architecture. Yet as rapidly as Louis Sullivan's reputation rose toward the turn of the century, it sub-

Opposite: The Great Fire in Chicago in 1871.

Above: Albert and Louis Sullivan as children.

The Sullivans' first child was a stillborn daughter, their second a boy whom they named Albert. Their third and last child, born on September 3, 1856, on the second floor of 22 South Bennett Street in Boston, Massachusetts, was called Louis Henry. (He eventually changed the spelling to Henri and spoke his first name with a French pronunciation, as if spelled Louee.)

Andrienne List, Louis' mother, was 21 when Louis was born. Her father, Henri List, was German, a highly educated, humorous man. Her mother, Anna, was Swiss-French, born in Geneva. The couple had owned a linen and lace shop in the Old Country and had been prosperous at first, but unwise speculation had led to financial disaster, and, with money borrowed from Anna's relatives, they, too, had left Europe for the New World. The Bennett Street address of Louis's birth was the List home, for the Sullivans had moved in with them shortly before he was born.

Young Louis had a phenomenal memory. Even his infancy was vivid to him in later years – clear visual images accompanied equally sharp emotion. He recollected singing to his grandmother about giants and fairies as she bathed him. He recorded his raptures as he toddled underneath the piano while his mother played Chopin. He watched through a window as the street was cobblestoned and the sidewalk coursed in brick.

Once, on the dusty road to school, he was overwhelmed by a giant ash tree, transfixed by its grandeur. Later, exploring a ravine, he followed a rivulet to a meadow and saw a tall, slender, beautiful elm tree. The exaltation of his recollected reverie, in which the ash has a male presence and the elm female, seems almost pantheistic and anticipates his later philosophical and spiritual orientation.

Louis's mother and father moved out of the Bennett Street house and changed their addresses frequently. The Lists also moved, taking up residence on a farm near Boston for a time. Louis spent part of his childhood going back and forth between the two households. Though he wrote unkindly of his father, he also described their close relationship, acknowledging his father's passion for "scenery." Louis enjoyed their outings together, including the rigorous physical exercise his father insisted upon – 5 AM reveille, a cold drink of water from the town pump (they lived briefly in a hotel in the coastal town of Newburyport, north of Boston), a brisk two-mile jaunt and then a dip in the sea. Though his father's face was less than attractive, Louis was elegiac about Patrick's athletic prowess and physique, his "hairy chest, satiny white skin and quick flexible muscles over which the sunshine danced with each movement."

During one solitary excursion the little boy became terrified by a monstrous form looming ominously over the Merrimack River. Not only did his father come to the rescue and calm his fear, but with skill and patience explained the wonder of a suspension bridge. Then he took his son on outings to watch shipbuilding, and "the child was in seventh heaven; here were his beloved strong men, the workers – his idols."

sequently faded. Since his death at the age of 67 in 1924, his true value to the profession has been argued rather than secured. He died, a pauper and an alcoholic, in a hotel room.

Louis Sullivan's paternal grandfather, the story goes, was an Irish landscape painter and a widower who went from country fair to country fair with his only child, Patrick. At one of these fairs, when Patrick was 12 years old, his father lost him forever in a crowd. The barefoot boy, now on his own, continued traveling from town to town, but with a fiddle rather than a paint brush, playing for country dances. He ended up in London, where he himself learned to dance and began to teach dancing of all sorts, from the polka to classical ballet. On July 22, 1847, Patrick O'Sullivan sailed from London to Boston, where he opened a dancing academy. He was "unlovely in person," his son would later write, "his too-sloping shoulders, his excessive Irish face, his small repulsive eyes – the eyes of a pig – of nondescript color and no flash, sunk into his head under rough brows." Yet this did not prevent Patrick Sullivan from marrying a graceful young woman, 15 years younger than himself, who was an accomplished pianist and a potential business asset. "He may have loved her," Louis conceded. "It is possible but hardly probable; for there is nothing in the record to show that he loved others, or that he loved himself. He was merely self-centered – not even cold."

Left: Merrill Wheelock's neo-Gothic Second Masonic Temple, built at the NE corner of Tremont and Boylston Streets in Boston between 1865 and 1867.

Opposite: The Broad Street elevation of Furness and Hewett's Pennsylvania Academy of the Fine Arts, which was built in 1873 in Philadelphia.

In his autobiography Louis Sullivan sets the groundwork for his continuing love of nature, his admiration of physical beauty and the accomplishments of men, as well as his spiritual predispositions. In his early schooling he was often a reluctant, bored student who could excel when challenged. He went to Rice Grammar and then English High School in Boston and became familiar with the city and its suburbs. "Beadle's Dime Novels," melodramatic adventure stories, suddenly became popular, and Louis was a fan, thrilled by the hero's bold exploits. As to his brother, Alfred, Sullivan gives us no information about their childhood together, since they had an unreconciled falling out by the time Louis wrote about his early life.

At about the age of 12, Louis became interested in buildings, though more as personalities than as structures. One, in particular, inspired him. It was a light grey, hewn granite Masonic Temple on the northeast corner of Boston's Tremont and Boylston Streets. When he learned that "so beautiful a building" as this Masonic Temple "came out of a man's head," as he put it, he decided that architecture was his calling.

Without actually finishing high school – where Asa Gray's *School and Field Book of Botany* had been his "playground"

under the instruction of his first true academic mentor, Moses Woolson – Louis took an exam that admitted him to the Massachusetts Institute of Technology in October, 1872. He was 16 years old. In November of that year, exactly a year after Chicago's Great Fire, a terrible fire also engulfed Boston. Louis followed the flames with a mixture of terror and awe and, when it was over, was assigned, as a member of the MIT "battalion," to guard the streets.

Finding MIT too rigid and too repetitive of ancient canons, he left at the end of the school year and set off for Philadelphia, where his widowed grandfather List then lived. According to the story Sullivan later told, he looked at buildings, decided he liked a house on the west side of South Broad street, found out that architect Frank Furness had designed it and boldly secured a job in Furness's office. Some biographers dispute his reporting of that "coup" as too self-serving and suggest, rather, that Sullivan had letters of introduction, paving his way. In either case, the time Sullivan spent in Furness's prestigious firm rewarded him with valuable experience.

He might have stayed in Philadelphia, but by the end of that year a financial panic moved through the city with the rapidity of the fire he had witnessed in Boston. There was a run on the banks and business came to a halt. As the last person hired, young Sullivan was the first fired. He took the train for Chicago, where his parents had settled. He wrote of his own arrival: "Louis tramped the platform, stopped, looked toward the city, ruins around him; looked at the sky; and as one alone, stamped his foot, raised his hand and cried in full voice: "THIS IS THE PLACE FOR ME!"

Though it had been two years since the Great Fire and the re-building of Chicago was in full swing – it is said that the output of the city's architects was measured by the mile rather than the numbers of jobs – there were still vast areas in ashes or built up with makeshift shanties. One of Chicago's leading architects at this time was Major William Le Baron Jenney. Attracted by a new building of Jenney's, the seven-story Portland Block, Sullivan presented himself at the architect's office and secured a job.

Jenney had been trained at the *Ecole Polytechnique* in France and had served as an army engineer during the Civil War, accompanying General Sherman on his march to the sea in the fall of 1864. If Jenney's French was jarring to the ears of a Francophile like Sullivan (whose maternal grandparents were, after all, French-speaking), Jenney's epicurean taste in food and wine was some compensation, and his manner more so. He was a vivid presence in the office, friendly and generous, and his firm was the training ground for several architects, besides Louis Sullivan, whose names eventually became well known, Martin Roche and William Holabird among them.

During his first six month sojourn in Chicago working for Jenney, Sullivan developed an important friendship with the office foreman, John Edelmann. Edelmann was several years older than Sullivan, who admired him greatly for his athletic abilities, his artistic accomplishments and his intellectual depth. Besides all that, his new friend was full of antic fun: "In [Jenney's] absences, which were frequent and long, bedlam reigned. John Edelmann would mount a drawing table and make a howling stump speech on greenback currency, or single tax, while at the same time Louis, at the top of his voice, sang selections from oratorios, beginning with his favorite, "Why do the Nations So Furiously Rage Together?" Sullivan wrote of the "joyous deviltry" that ended when the office lookout warned "Cheeseit, cullies; the Boss!"

Sullivan's professional resolve interrupted his good times at Jenney's office, for he set sail from New York on July 11, 1874, en route to study in Paris at the *Ecole Nationale et Spéciale des Beaux-Arts*. The institutional origin of this most prestigious

school could be traced back to 1671, and its spiritual origins beyond that to concepts that evolved during the Italian Renaissance, the very beginning of formal architecture. In the nineteenth century it was the world center for architectural education, of which MIT had been a mere satellite. Henry Hobson Richardson had studied there, as had most of America's important architects, if not in person then as students of another of the country's leading designers, Richard Morris Hunt. Their stories of *Ecole* escapades, personalities and ideas had fired Sullivan's imagination.

Once in Paris he engaged tutors to brush up his French and mathematics for the examinations he would need to pass in order to enter the *Ecole*. Thus, to his fondly-remembered Moses Woolson, whose strict discipline he always appreciated as having taught him self-discipline and self-reliance, he now added another influential teacher, one Monsieur Clopet.

Regarding the books Sullivan had brought to his first tutorial class, Clopet made a comment that instantly became engraved in the young man's mind. "Now observe," he said, turning the pages of a book on descriptive geometry, "here is a problem with five exceptions or special cases; here a theorem, three special cases; another, nine; and so on and so on, a procession of exceptions and special cases. I suggest you place the book in the waste basket; we shall not need it here; for here our demonstrations shall be so broad as to admit of NO EXCEPTION!"

The powerful influence these words – or, more accurately, the idea behind them – had on Sullivan is probably inestimable. He vowed to devote his life to finding and upholding similar absolute principles in architecture. In his own view, that is doubtless how he proceeded through his subsequent career, discovering truths that admitted of no exceptions, but others would be less convinced.

Examinations passed with distinction, Sullivan traveled briefly, then returned to Paris and his studies. Although we have no formal record of these, typically 20 or so students worked in an atelier under the tutelage of a patron, each on a specific building problem assigned to him. But we do know that, in addition, Sullivan also received a commission from home via his friend John Edelmann, who had left Jenney's office and was then working independently with a partner. For Edelmann he sketched ornamental fresco designs that show his sustained interest in intricate plant forms. Though the buildings they decorated have been torn down, the sketches are preserved.

In due course he finished his work at the *Ecole* and returned to Chicago even fuller of ambition, of the possibilities of architecture and of the transcendent value of his own ideas than when he left America. One thing which he did *not* bring back was any commitment to the current academic fashion in building, known as the Beaux Arts style, of which he had seen more than enough. Before long his rejection of all that Beaux Arts represented would become outspoken.

At the time of Sullivan's return on May 24, 1875, the countrywide depression had caught up with Chicago, and the

building industry was slow. He worked as a freelance for various offices, and, over the course of time was introduced to a successful architect named Dankmar Adler, by his friend Edelmann. The introduction led to a professional association and eventually to a partnership that would last 14 years, during which Adler would be increasingly concerned with the engineering, and Sullivan with the artistic design, of their projects.

The most popular styles of the time were represented by buildings such as the gaudy, quasi-Second Empire Palmer House hotel designed by John Mills Van Osdel. Rudyard Kipling called it "a gilded and mirrored rabbit-warren" and described "a huge hall of tessellated marble, crammed with people talking about money and spitting about everywhere. Other barbarians charged in and out of this inferno with letters and telegrams in their hands, and yet others shouted at each other. A man who had drunk quite as much as was good for him told me this was the finest hotel in the finest city on God Almighty's earth." The dismissive tone of the English author's architectural critique may not have been shared by many Chicagoans, but it certainly was shared by Sullivan.

The depression eventually passed, rebuilding in Chicago resumed and by the 1880s architectural ideas that owed nothing to the inspiration that had produced the Palmer house were beginning to take physical form. Major Jenney was one whose combined engineering and architectural prowess lead many today to credit him with the invention of the first skyscraper – his 10-story Home Insurance Building of 1885. Previously, the height of buildings relied on the thickness of the foundation walls supporting them, and to go to any substantial height the bearing walls had to be incrementally, and generally prohibitively, thick. But Jenney found an entirely different solution: iron and steel.

A number of architects had earlier experimented with the use of cast and wrought iron for support, but it was Jenney – who used metal as the entire skeletal support of his Home Insurance Building – who is usually credited with bringing the techinque to fruition. Subsequently, Chicago became known as birthplace of the tall commercial building, and the group of architects competing and cooperating to design these buildings is now called the "Chicago School." The best known among them during the last quarter of the nineteenth century were William Le Baron Jenney himself, Daniel H. Burnham, John Wellborn Root, William Holabird, Martin Roche, Dankmar Adler and his partner Louis Henri Sullivan.

Not a member of the Chicago School, but an architect who influenced many of these Chicago designers in terms of style, was the Boston-based Henry Hobson Richardson, whose Brattle Street (Cambridge) church had impressed the young Sullivan even more than his better known Trinity Church (Boston). From Richardson's renowned drafting table came two houses for Chicago (one of which, the Glessner house, is

Opposite: Dankmar Adler, the Chicago architect who would become Louis Sullivan's partner in 1880.

Above: Trinity Church in Boston's Copley Square, designed by Henry Hobson Richardson.

Below: A sketch of the Newburyport Bridge made in 1868 by Patrick Sullivan, Louis Sullivan's father. Louis had an ambiguous love-hate relationship with his father, but apparently inherited Patrick's artistic talent.

Above: Chicago's John J. Glessner House, typical of H.H. Richardson's neo-Romanesque style.

Left: An interior view from the Glessner House's front door.

Opposite: The Marshall Field Wholesale Store of 1895 was one of the few Richardson designs to which Sullivan gave his wholehearted approval.

considered his most beautiful residential design), as well as a new Marshall Field Wholesale Store. The latter demonstrates Richardson's characteristic rusticated stone and arched windows. Though the facades of his buildings were reminiscent of ponderous, eleventh-century Romanesque cathedrals, they carried forward a unique Americanization in their roughness and horizontality.

The name that was on Richardson's lips when he died at the age of 48 in 1886 was that of Chicago merchant Marshall Field, for Field's unfinished seven-story granite building was then foremost on the architect's mind. It was also on the minds of many Chicagoans, including John Root and Daniel Burnham, who would be inspired by it in their design of their office block

called The Rookery in 1888. It may even have been a low-rise preamble to the Monadnock building, a 16-story-high non-steel structure which, when it was built in 1891, was the tallest commercial building in the world. But influential though the Field building may have been, it was essentially one of the last of the old-style buildings, with 12-foot masonry supporting walls at street level. It would be Jenney's inspiration, not Richardson's, that would prove critical to the Chicago School.

Although Burnham and Root were the primary competitors of Adler and Sullivan, another notable Chicago partnership was that of Holabird and Roche. Their Tacoma Office Building in Chicago, built in 1887-88, competes with Jenney's Home Insurance Building for the title of first skyscraper in Chicago.

Sullivan himself is one who credits Holabird and Roche with being the first to apply the steel-frame construction method, but he quickly goes on to say that the genre received its first "authentic recognition and expression in the exterior treatment of the Wainwright Building" – Sullivan's own creation.

It is certainly true that the architect who ultimately developed the most distinctive treatment for tall buildings was Louis Henri Sullivan. He saw the problem of taking structures ever higher as the most important challenge to architects of his era. Yet in his and Adler's first major commission, the building that won them fame when it opened at the end of 1889, they were still not yet using the innovative steel-frame construction.

Preliminary sketches for this enormous building – then the heaviest and most massive in the world – were begun in 1886, when Sullivan was 30 years old and Adler 42. It covered over 1½ acres, rose first 10 stories high and then soared another six stories in a bold, eloquent tower. It housed a 400-room hotel, a

business section with offices and stores and a 4200-seat theater, the largest permanent concert hall ever built. The complex, which stands today fronting on Chicago's Michigan Boulevard, is known as the Auditorium Building. It was the city's biggest sensation since the Great Fire.

Through previous commissions, Adler had earned acolades for designing halls with superlative acoustics and unobstructed sight lines for the entire audience. His engineering skills were magnificently expressed, too, in the support system he designed for this mammoth Auditorium project. Sullivan's innovative design of facades and interiors were extravagantly praised. On the lower floors of the Auditorium the thick rusticated stone walls, with their arched entrance and windows, were inspired by Richardsonian Romanesque, but the inside was pure Sullivan. Even the painted landscapes contained inscriptions from his own obscure poem, "Inspiration": "O, soft, melodious Springtime! First-born of life and love!" and, "A great life has passed into the tomb, and there, awaits the requiem of Winter's snows."

Ornamentation was to Sullivan much more than the complexity and beauty recognized by most who praised his geometric, floral and foliate pattern. To him these designs represented a philosophical belief. It was his conviction that man, the hero – athlete, street-paver, bridge-builder – must surrender his individual will to the supreme will of nature. Sullivan wanted his buildings to remind people of their bond to nature and to find sublime joy in that attachment. He also believed that internal beauty is reflected externally and what is seen on the outside is a clear representation of what lies beneath the surface. And he was committed to the idea that the aesthetic environment shapes human behavior. In such transcendental terms – inspired in part by Walt Whitman, his favorite poet, and the German philosopher Nietzsche – Louis Sullivan expressed his deepest motives as an architect. He was an evangelist, a proselytizer, a master builder intent upon saving the world.

Salvation, to both Sullivan and Whitman, depended upon the success of a true American democracy. Not the political democracy of the time, nowhere more corrupt than in the city of his architectural practice, but a democracy in harmony with the laws and aesthetics of nature that only the poet/artist could make manifest. As the artists of the era just before, as well as during, Sullivan's years of design – Thomas Cole, Frederic Church, Asher Durand, for example – celebrated the majesty of the American landscape on their canvases, so did Sullivan mandate an indigenous American architecture. It should be based, he insisted, not upon the classic Beaux Arts modes of the Old World, or on any other derivative style, but rather on the natural, vital, organic forms of America itself.

Nowadays the chief objection to large-scale steel-box construction is its lack of humanity. But this may be a post-Bauhaus perception. Certainy it was not Sullivan's. Steel frame construction allowed him to bring ever more light into the interiors of tall buildings. And he lavished decoration on them inside and out, with the very offerings of nature that give people the most pleasure: flowers. His buildings, no matter how high and potentially overbearing, were meant never in any way to diminish the men and women who worked in them; they should be friendly and comfortable and bring pleasure. But more than that, the idealistic Sullivan truly believed that when people at last realized the meaning of his architecture, their very lives would be changed into something richer and, in the end, more noble.

Recognizing Louis Sullivan's behavior as an expression of these beliefs, it is easier to undertand why he would admit no exceptions and brook no accommodation. And his later behavior, which at first glance seems pig-headed and self-defeating, becomes somewhat more understandable. Visionaries are notoriously unable to compromise. Yet at the time, almost nobody knew what he was doing, or what he was talking about in his incessant, convoluted, metaphorical writings. As one of his former professors, to whom he had sent a poem, replied, "The language is beautiful, but what on earth you are talking about I have not the faintest idea."

The Auditorium Building took nearly four years of driving, exhausting work, at the end of which both Adler and Sullivan collapsed. Sullivan traveled to the West Coast and on his way back east stopped in Ocean Springs, Mississippi, just outside Biloxi, to see some friends. While there, he bought beachfront land on the Gulf of Mexico and built a cottage. Although it was a long commute from Chicago, it became his vacation refuge. He usually headed south in October, and he became a devoted gardener, especially passionate about his roses.

During the 1880s and early 1890s the firm of Adler and Sullivan was famous, and commissions flowed in. Besides private residences, a mainstay of the practice for many years, their success with the Auditorium Building brought many large-scale commissions, among them the Chicago Stock Exchange, the Wainwright building in Saint Louis, the Guaranty building in Buffalo, the Bayard Building in New York City and the Schlesinger Meyer Department Store of Chicago, later known as the Carson Pirie Scott building. During this period Sullivan's designs moved steadily away from the influence of Richardson, and his facades became ever lighter, with more elaborate yet more delicate ornamentation.

Adler and Sullivan had moved their offices into the tower of their own Auditorium Building, and their staff had grown to as many as 50 employees. Among them was a young man with obviously enormous talent, Frank Lloyd Wright. Sullivan became Wright's "Master," and as a disciple Wright would carry forth the notion of an indigenous American architecture, an organic, natural blending not only of form and function, but also of form and its environment – the natural landscape – a unique melding of the man-made and natural worlds.

Wright was just one of the younger architects influenced by Sullivan's beliefs. Sullivan's effect on this group – Wright, George Mahar, Walter Burly Griffin, William Purcell and George Elmslie, primarily – has led some architectural historians to designate *them* the "Chicago School," rather than the very different group – made up of Sullivan's peers – who are popularly acknowledged under that heading.

Regardless of his label or affiliation, it was one of Sullivan's peers, his good friend John Root, who may indirectly have contributed to the beginning of Sullivan's professional downfall. In 1890 Root was put in charge of architectural planning for the

Opposite: A contender for the title of "Chicago's First Modern Skyscraper" was the Tacoma Building, designed by Holabird and Roche in 1887. It was torn down in 1929.

Right: The stables that Sullivan designed for his summer residence in Ocean Springs, Mississippi.

1893 World's Columbian Exposition, also known as the Chicago World's Fair and as the White City (because of the predominant color of the architecture). Root promoted the idea of bringing in outside architects, and 10 of the nation's top firms were selected for the Board of Architects, five from Chicago – Adler and Sullivan, William Le Baron Jenney, Henry Ives Cobb, Charles S. Frost and Burling & Whitehouse. The remaining five were outside firms; from New York, Richard Morris Hunt, George B. Post, McKim, Mead & White; from Boston, Peabody and Stearns; and from Kansas City, Ware & Van Brunt.

John Root is likely to have been Sullivan's ally on the board, but he died prematurely, before the major decisions were made, and that left Sullivan to face the powerful eastern establishment alone, since Burnham and the rest seemed entirely deferential to the big names from Boston and New York. Despite Sullivan's heated protests and virulent criticism, the program that was developed called for the very kind of architecture he hated most to see in America, let alone in Chicago, buildings with pillars and pediments in the classical Roman idiom.

The damage wrought by the Fair's architecture on the American psyche may have been grievous from Sullivan's perspective, but the people loved it. As a result, the more he complained about the Fair in public – which he did often and at length – the more his reputation suffered in the United States. On the other hand, his own contribution to the Fair, the Transportation Building, was so highly regarded abroad that a

Sullivan's problems at this period were personal as well as professional. Albert, Louis's older brother, married in 1893, and it is generally thought that Albert's wife caused the estrangement that separated the two men. They had been close, both living in Chicago, and Albert, a railroad executive, had probably been helpful to the architectural firm in gaining a few commissions. That the separation was painful can only be assumed from the fact that Louis never mentions his brother in his autobiography. But it is known that Albert was deeply affected by his brother's death.

Louis Sullivan's private life is another matter open to speculation. He did not marry until 1899, when he was nearly 43, though it was rumored he had had affairs with two women before that. In general he was a congenial guest, a willing pianist and a voluble, if sometimes overbearing, conversationalist. Very little is known about his wife, Margaret. She was tall and had dark brown eyes and brown hair fastened in a pompadour. They married on July 1, 1899. She rode out 10 years of his professional decline, then left him at the end of 1909.

Though he did design some very important buildings after the partnership broke up, they were few. His Bayard building in New York City (1897), and the banks he did in the West, especially the one in Owatonna, Minnesota (1906), were among his masterpieces. But often, when a much-needed job was offered him, Sullivan would alienate his clients with his arrogant, uncompromising attitude and lose the commission. No doubt his heavy drinking made matters worse: "Idle days are hard to bear," he told his only remaining assistant, George Elmslie. Finally, when there were no more buildings to design, Sullivan was reduced to writing and giving lectures.

There was a reconciliation with Wright, and there were, until the end, colleagues who visited him from time to time: he was forced to sell almost everything he owned and had to ask Wright and others for financial help. He worked diligently on his autobiography and lived just long enough to see it to publication – his final pleasure.

Louis Henri Sullivan died in Chicago, in his sleep, early on the morning of April 14, 1924, of heart and kidney disease. He was 67 years old. His health had been in decline for some time, and his death was not unexpected. Although he was an important member of the well known Chicago School of skyscraper builders, in fact his influence on them was less than enduring.

But Sullivan did have another group of followers whom he influenced profoundly. It is through these architects, who have also come to be known, in professional circles at least, as the Chicago School, that Sullivan's impact on the profession has been most permanent and creative. It is not so much in their style of building that they reveal their debt to his philosophy. Rather it is in their *approach* to design, in their recognition of the idea that form must follow function, that they carry on his artistic bequest. This is a more subtle heritage, more difficult to identify than immediately recognizable styles such as Neo-Classic, Bauhaus or even Beaux-Arts – but it is also a good deal more significant.

Opposite top: The Chicago Exhibition of 1893. The low dark building in the upper left is Sullivan's Transportation Building.

Opposite below: Margaret Sullivan, Louis's only wife. Their marriage was not a success.

Above: Frank Lloyd Wright was Sullivan's assistant at Adler & Sullivan. In later years Wright would always refer to Sullivan as "The Master", and it was plain that the term meant more to Wright than just an allusion to his days as an apprentice.

cast of its Golden Door and model of the building itself were made for a museum in Paris.

The year the Fair opened, 1893, was also a year in which another major recession cut severely into all building. Just before that, moreover, Sullivan had discovered that Wright, his protegé, had been moonlighting, accepting small design commissions and executing them secretly, since it was against his contractual arrangement with the firm to take outside work. The deception enraged Sullivan and not only led to Wright's dismissal, but also added to the tensions between Sullivan and Adler that had earlier developed when Adler wanted to bring his sons into the firm. Now the partnership broke up under the additional strains created by the economic downturn.

AFTER THE FIRE: THE CHICAGO SCHOOL

The Great Fire of 1871 razed downtown Chicago as effectively as an army of bulldozers on a rampage. But even before all the debris was cleared rebuilding had begun. New technologies developing in Philadelphia and New York, as well as in Chicago, led to skeleton framing, primarily in iron and steel, a technique that allowed buildings to climb ever higher. Previously, a building's height had been limited by the massiveness of its stone foundations. The tallest building constructed in the old-fashioned mode was also in Chicago: Burnham and Root's 1891 Monadnock Building, 16 stories high.

Chicago became known as the birthplace the tall commercial building that is called the skyscraper. Other important advances enabling skyscraper construction included the elevator (invented some years before, but now proving its potential) and methods of fireproofing. "The architects of Chicago welcomed the steel frame and did something with it. The architects of the East were appalled by it and could make no contribution," wrote Louis Sullivan. Certainly, it can be said that what happened in Chicago during the last quarter of the nineteenth century – especially the skyscraper boom from 1890-1893 – changed the look of buildings all over the world.

Who was the first to build a real skyscraper? The jury is still out. William Le Baron Jenney's 10-story Home Insurance Building (1883-85) is most often cited. Jenney, the son of a wealthy New Bedford, Massachusetts, shipowner, had impressive social standing and an excellent education before he moved to Chicago in 1868. He is judged an engineer more than an architect, an international businessman more than a designer. (His position on the staff of General Sherman during the Civil War earned him the title of Major, and it fit his colorful personality.) Among other contenders for the title of building the first skyscraper were William Holabird and and Martin Roche, for their 13-story Tacoma Building (1886-1889). But if the argument over who was first becomes academic, there is no denying that Sullivan's artistic treatments of the skyscraper eclipsed those of all other designers.

The greatest opportunity Sullivan might have had to express his ideas was the World Columbian Exhibition, or World's Fair, scheduled to take place in Chicago in 1893. Authorized by an Act of Congress in 1890, the Fair was planned to commemorate the 400th anniversary of the discovery of America by Christopher Columbus. It was to be the ultimate showplace for the latest and best cultural offerings from around the world. "The site," as Sullivan wrote, "was to be transformed and embellished by the magic of American prowess, particularly in its architectural aspects. . . . It was to be a dream city, where one might revel in beauty. It was to be called The White City by the Lake."

To most people it was all it was supposed to be, but to Louis Sullivan it was a disaster. Despite the vehemence with which he railed against the architecture of the eastern establishment, they prevailed. The Beaux Arts buildings they loved – with heavy stone bases, grand stairways, columns, pediments, decorative swags, medallions, sculptural figures – lined the streets, and the crowds loved it. Perhaps the most enduring invention unveiled at the Fair, the Ferris Wheel, is symbolic of what was happening in architecture: like the eastern architects' stylistic recycling, it went round and round.

Sullivan predicted, "The damage wrought by the World's Fair will last for half a century." But he was too pessimistic. His young followers, some of whom had been his employees, carried on his ideas. Of those influenced by Sullivan, Frank Lloyd Wright is by far the best known. But the great Finnish architect, Eliel Saarinen, father of Eero Saarinen, also found inspiration in Sullivan's example. When Saarinen's entry in the competition for design of the Chicago Tribune Tower in 1923 did not win, Sullivan wrote a letter of outrage to the newspaper. The entry chosen resembled the tower of a Gothic cathedral rather than an office building for a daily newspaper.

Through the term "Chicago School" is generally applied to the men who pioneered the architecture of the high rise building, some scholars attach that label to the followers of the man who insisted that each building express its own individuality, that it be an expression of the concept that form must follow function. Fortunately, the latter Chicago School eventually gained its foothold in design.

William Le Baron Jenney
Home Insurance Building, 1885,
Chicago, IL, demolished.
Photo: The Bettmann Archive

Henry Ives Cobb
Potter Palmer Mansion, 1882,
Chicago, IL, demolished 1950.
Photo: The Bettmann Archive

Burnham & Root
Flatiron Building, 1902,
New York, NY.
Photo: Brompton Photo Library

Burnham & Root
*The Art Institute on Michigan
Ave. (later The Chicago Club),
1884-85, Chicago, IL, demolished
1929.*
Photo: Courtesy of the Chicago
Historical Society

Burnham & Root
Women's Christian Temperance Union, 1891, Chicago, IL, demolished 1926.
Photo: Clarence Fuermann
© The Chicago Architectural Photographing Co./David R. Phillips

Burnham & Root
Monadnock Building, 1889-91,
Chicago, IL.
Photo: The Bettmann Archive

Burnham & Root
The Rookery, 1886, Chicago, IL.
Photo: Clarence Fuermann
© The Chicago Architectural
Photographing Co./David R.
Phillips

Right:
*The Rookery, interior (remodeled
by Frank Lloyd Wright between
1905 and 1907).*
Photo: © Hedrich-Blessing

Holabird & Roche
The University Club, staircase,
1908-11, Chicago, IL.
Photo: © Hedrich-Blessing

*The University Club, The
Michigan Room.*
Photo: © Hedrich-Blessing

*The University Club, the dining
room.
Photo: © Hedrich-Blessing*

Holabird & Roche
LaSalle Hotel, The Blue Room,
1908, Chicago, IL.
Photo: © Hedrich-Blessing

Holabird & Roche
Chicago Board of Trade,
perspective sketch, 1927-30,
Chicago, IL.
Photo: The Bettmann Archive

Holabird & Roche
*No. 333 N. Michigan (Wirtz
Building), 1927-28, Chicago, IL.*
Photo: © Hedrich-Blessing

Left:
Holabird & Roche
Michigan Square Building, Diana
Court, 1930, Chicago, IL,
demolished 1973
Photo: © Hedrich-Blessing

World's Columbian Exhibition,
1893, South Basin from
Machinery Building, Chicago, IL.
Photo: The Bettmann Archive

World's Columbian Exposition,
Court of Honor.
Photo: The Bettmann Archive

IDEAS IN STONE AND STEEL

Louis Henri Sullivan was rewarded with success when he was young: he was just 26 when he became a principal in the firm of Adler & Sullivan. In the next two years he became a founding member of the Western Association of Architects and the Illinois State Association of Architects. The Auditorium Building brought him and his partner worldwide fame when he was still only 33. His star rose quickly.

Adler and Sullivan made no claim for pioneering in the construction techniques of skyscrapers; rather, their work concentrated on exploring the possibilities of steel-box structures. In 1896 Sullivan expressed his ideas in an essay entitled "The Tall Office Building Artistically Considered."

Problem: How shall we impart to this sterile pile, this crude, harsh, brutal agglomeration, this stark, staring exclamation of external strive, the graciousness of those higher forms of sensibility and culture . . . ? How shall we proclaim from the dizzy height of this strange, weird, modern housetop the peaceful evangel of sentiment, of beauty, the cult of a higher life? . . . It is my belief that it is of the very essence of every problem that it contains and suggests its own solution. This I believe to be natural law. . . . Whether it be the sweeping eagle in his flight or the open apple-blossom, the toiling work-horse, the blithe swan, the branching oak, the winding stream at its base, the drifting clouds, over all the coursing sun, form ever follows function, and this is the law.

During his architectural career – that is from 1876 to 1922 – Sullivan executed some 238 designs. As a principal in the firm of Adler & Sullivan, from May 1883 through June 1895, his name went on 158 projects. Not all, but a large number of them, were built. Today, only about 50 of Sullivan's buildings remain standing, and a number of these have been altered drastically. There is an irony in the fact that architecture, a medium of stone, bricks and metals, the strongest and most durable of materials, is such a perishable art form: painting and sculpture often seem to have a better chance for survival. It is certainly the case that the disappointments Sullivan experienced in life are painfully compounded by the loss of so many of the buildings he created. Although his professional reputation is now restored, there is, in general, no way to reconstruct his vanished buildings. One welcome exception, however, is that the Chicago Art Institute (housed in a building in the Classical style Sullivan rejected) has rebuilt – in full scale – parts of the Adler-Sullivan Chicago Stock Exchange as an exhibit.

Drawings and old photographs allow us to grasp his concepts, but we can only guess at the total effect created by most of those lost buildings. The Transportation Building he designed for the World's Fair, for example, must have provided a memorable experience. It was long and low, with 13 arched windows on either side of the imposing entrance, called the "Golden Door," which had five receding arches. This astonishing door was profusely ornamented with gold leaf and warm hues of red, orange and yellow. The long walls of the vast exhibition space beyond the door were splendidly colored in shades of ultramarine blue, red, orange, yellow and dark green. In it were settings appropriate for all the exhibitions, from Conestoga Wagon to hot air balloon, models of the first railway cars and the like. There were even four vast sheds, each containing an entire train. As one chronicler has commented, he had created a kind of horizontal skyscraper.

After the firm of Adler & Sullivan was dissolved, Sullivan had few requests for large commercial buildings, but regardless of the size of his commission, he executed the smallest details as if he were ornamenting a palace.

Louis Sullivan
*Chicago Stock Exchange Building,
arch and pool, 1894, Chicago, IL.*
Photo: © Robert Frerck/
Odyssey

Louis Sullivan
Auditorium Building (Roosevelt University), 1886-90, Chicago, IL.
Photo: © Hedrich-Blessing

Auditorium Building, theater.
Photo: © Hedrich-Blessing

Auditorium Building, lobby.
Photo: Clarence Fuermann
ⓒ The Chicago Architectural
Photographing Co./David R.
Phillips

Left:
Auditorium Building, theater.
Photo: ⓒ Cervin Robinson

45

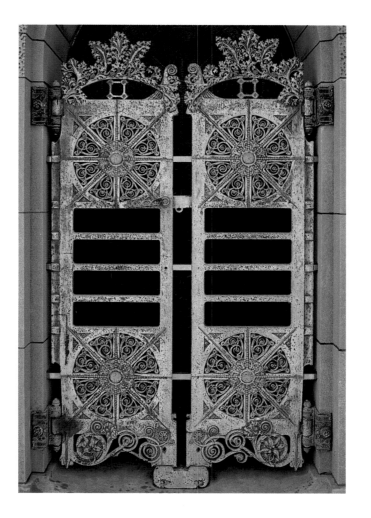

Left:
Louis Sullivan
Holy Trinity Orthodox Cathedral,
1903, Chicago, IL.
Photo: © Balthazar Korab Ltd.

Top:
Louis Sullivan
Carrie Eliza Getty Tomb,
Graceland Cemetery, 1890,
Chicago, IL.
Photo: © Gary Quesada/
Balthazar Korab Ltd.

Left:
Getty Tomb, bronze doors.
Photo: © Balthazar Korab Ltd.

Louis Sullivan
J.H. McVickers Theater,
1884-85, Chicago, IL, destroyed
by fire, 1890.
Photo: The Bettmann Archive

Right:
J.H. McVickers Theater,
remodeled, 1890.
Photo: The Bettmann Archive

Louis Sullivan
Wainwright Building, 1890,
St. Louis, MO.
Photo: © Jack Zehrt

Wainwright Building, atrium.
Photo: © Jack Zehrt

Louis Sullivan
James Charnley Residence, 1890,
Ocean Springs, MS.
Photo: © Scott McDonald/
Hedrich-Blessing

Right:
Charnley Residence, entryway.
Photo: © Nick Merrick/
Hedrich-Blessing

Louis Sullivan
Transportation Building, the
World's Columbian Exposition,
1893, Chicago, IL, demolished.
Photo: Clarence Fuermann
© The Chicago Architectural
Photographing Co./David R.
Phillips

The Golden Door, Transportation Building, The World's Columbian Exposition.
Photo: Clarence Fuermann
© The Chicago Architectural
Photographing Co./David R.
Phillips

Louis Sullivan
Guaranty Building, (Prudential Building), 1894-95, Buffalo, NY.
Photo: Patricia Layman Bazelon/Restoration by Cannon of Buffalo

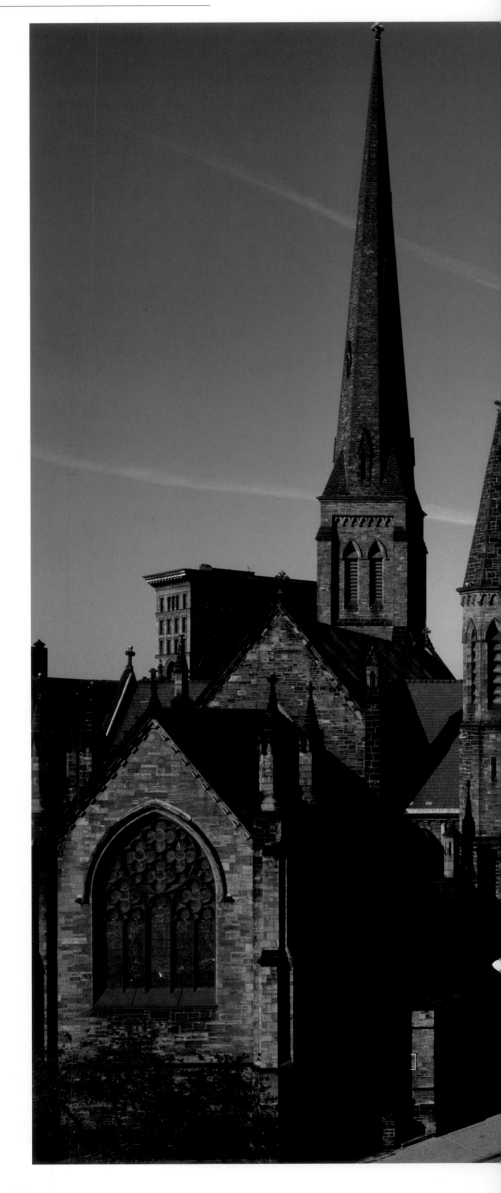

Left:
Guaranty Building, facade detail.
Photo: Patricia Layman
Bazelon/Restoration by Cannon
of Buffalo

*Guaranty Building, elevator
lobby.*
Photo: Patricia Layman
Bazelon/Restoration by Cannon
of Buffalo

59

Guaranty Building, foyer.
Photo: Patricia Layman
Bazelon/Restoration by Cannon
of Buffalo

Left:
Louis Sullivan
Schlesinger Meyer Store (Carson Pirie Scott Department Store), 1899-1904, Chicago, IL.
Photo: © Hedrich-Blessing

Above:
Schlesinger Meyer Store, facade detail.
Photo: © Balthazar Korab Ltd.

Schlesinger Meyer Store, entrance.
Photo: © Robert Frerck/ Odyssey

Right:
Louis Sullivan
Bayard Building (Condict Building), 1897, New York, NY.
Photo: The Wurt Brothers, The Wurts Collection, Museum of the City of New York

SULLIVAN IN DETAIL: THE SPIRIT OF ORNAMENT

"Over all he wove a web of beautiful ornament – flowers and frost, delicate as lace and strong as steel," is how one of Sullivan's admirers described the master's ornamental touch.

During his high school days Asa Gray's *School and Field Book of Botany* absorbed Louis Sullivan's interest. Later he studied and traced Victor-Marie Ruprich-Robert's *Flore ornementale*, a volume of plates showing decorative abstractions of plant types and how they could be elaborated in painted and carved ornamentation. Finally, just before he died, he completed his own manifesto, *A System of Architectural Ornament According with a Philosophy of Man's Powers*, which was published posthumously.

It begins with the drawing of a winged seed pod, like that of a maple tree, and, under the heading "The Germ: The Seat of Power," the text begins:

> Above is drawn a diagram of a typical seed with the two cotyledons. The cotyledons are specialized rudimentary leaves containing a supply of nourishment sufficient for the initial stage of the development of the germ.
>
> The Germ is the real thing: the seat of identity. Within its delicate mechanism lies the will to power: the function of which is to seek and eventually find its full expression in form.
>
> The seat of power and the will to life constitute the simple working idea upon which all that follows is based. . . .

The more one looks at Sullivan's details, the more astounding it seems that the man could have conceived of such complex, elegant, mysterious shapes, one growing out of another, linking, curling, looping back, dividing, multiplying. Sometimes the designs are laid down in layers, and it is fascinating to trace the superimpositions. When possible, he was fully as attentive to color as he was to sculptural detail. It seems safe to say that Sullivan's eye for the possibilities of architectural ornamentation has never been surpassed.

Not all Sullivan's ornamentation is elaborate. The repetitive design on the Getty Tomb, for example, a motif with Islamic references, is a pattern of repeated octagons with a starburst in the center. The tomb is simple and elegant, massive and delicate, at the same time, alluding to eternal protection with a light hand.

The loss of the majority of Sullivan's buildings has meant the loss of much of his "flowers and frost" ornamentation. Not all, however. There are a number of examples preserved by the Art Institute of Chicago, but the greatest collection is at Southern Illinois University at Edwardsville. In the early 1960s John D. Randall, former campus architect, and John C. Lovejoy, director of the Lovejoy Library, had the foresight to enlist the help of Richard Nickel, an architectural historian and photographer. Nickel set about identifying buildings that were scheduled to be torn down and negotiated with owners, wrecking companies, unions and workmen for help in salvaging pieces of ornament. This he did for nearly 20 years.

The university then undertook to restore this treasure trove, removing accumulated layers of dirt and paint and reproducing as nearly as possible the original appearance. The fortunate result is several hundred restored pieces from 28 buildings – residences, a library, theaters, office buildings, stores and banks. Included are pediments, door panels, newel posts, ceiling screens and panels, elevator grilles and pushplates, kickplates, light fixtures, windows, chimneys, friezes and even some stenciled wallpaper. The major works are on permanent display in the Sullivan gallery, and they are being added to as restoration proceeds. The total effect is dazzling.

Guaranty Building, facade detail.
Photo: Patricia Layman
Bazelon/Restoration by Cannon
of Buffalo

Above:
Louis Sullivan
Gage Building, spandrel fascia panel from facade, 1889-99, Chicago, IL.
Photo: John Gronkowski
© The Art Institute of Chicago. All rights reserved

Top right:
Schlesinger Meyer Store (Carson Pirie Scott Department Store), Sullivan's initials in bronze facade.
Photo: © Robert Frerck/ Odyssey

Bottom right:
Louis Sullivan
J.D. Van Allen and Co. Dry-Goods Store, facade detail, 1913-15, Clinton, IA.
Photo: Courtesy of the Southern Illinois University Museum

Auditorium Building, theater interior.
Photo: © Wayne Andrews/ ESTO

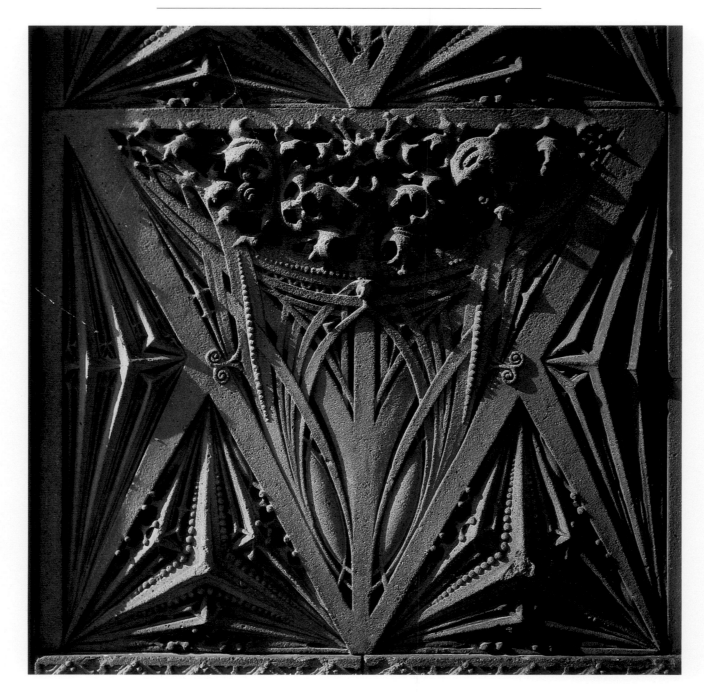

Above:
Guaranty Building, facade detail.
Photo: © Balthazar Korab Ltd.

Right:
Wainwright Building.
Photo: © Jack Zehrt

Louis Sullivan
Chicago Stock Exchange, painted stencil from Trading Room, 1893-94.
Photo: © Hedrich-Blessing

Chicago Stock Exchange, painted stencil from Trading Room. Photo: © Hedrich-Blessing

Above:
Louis Sullivan
*Martin Barbe Residence, panel
assembly, 1884, Chicago, IL.*
Photo: Courtesy of the
Southern Illinois University
Museum

Right:
Louis Sullivan
*Henry Stern Residence, door
panel, 1885, Chicago, IL.*
Photo: Courtesy of the
Southern Illinois University
Museum

Left:
*Guaranty Building, interior
mosaic detail.*
Photo: Patricia Layman
Bazelon/Restoration by Cannon
of Buffalo

Chicago Stock Exchange,
kickplate.
Photo: Courtesy the Southern
Illinois University Museum

Above:
Martin Barbe Residence, lunette.
Photo: Courtesy the Southern
Illinois University Museum

Below:
Louis Sullivan
*Braunstein Building, frieze, 1894,
Chicago, IL.*
Photo: Courtesy of the
Southern Illinois University
Museum

Right top:
Garrick Theater, "star pod."
Photo: Courtesy of the
Southern Illinois University
Museum

Louis Sullivan
*Garrick Theater, (Schiller
Theater), banquet hall frieze
panel, 1891-92, Chicago, IL.*
Photo: Courtesy of the
Southern Illinois University
Museum

Right below:
Louis Sullivan
*Henry Babson Residence,
terracotta decorative block, 1907,
Riverside, IL.*
Photo: Courtesy the Southern
Illinois University Museum

Left top:
Guaranty Building, facade detail.
Photo: Iris Cheney

Left below:
*Guaranty Building, column
detail.*
Photo: Iris Cheney

Louis Sullivan
*Union Trust Building, entrance,
1893, St. Louis, MO.*
Photo: Clarence Fuermann
© The Chicago Architectural
Photographing Co./David R.
Phillips

Louis Sullivan
*National Farmers Bank (Security
Bank & Trust Co.), interior,
stained glass window, 1906,
Owatonna, MN.*
Photo: A1 Ominsky/Minnesota
Historical Society

Right:
Louis Sullivan
*Merchants National Bank
(Brenton National Bank of
Poweshiek County), entrance,
1913-14, Grinnell, IA.*
Photo: Courtesy of Brenton
National Bank

Louis Sullivan
*People's Federal Savings & Loan
Association Bank, 1917, Sidney,
OH.*
Photo: © Balthazar Korab Ltd.

National Farmers Bank, interior detail.
Photo: A1 Ominsky/Minnesota Historical Society

Sullivan's Last Masterpiece

"I want a color symphony and I am pretty sure I am going to get it. . . . There has never been in my entire career such an opportunity for a color tone poem as your bank interior plainly puts before me," Louis Sullivan wrote to Carl Kent Bennett of Owatonna, Minnesota, on April 1, 1908.

Owatonna is in the valley of the Straight River, about 65 miles south of Minneapolis. The population in 1907 was 5500, and the outstanding distinction of the town was that it boasted 21 creameries. It was said that the 16 square miles around Owatonna produced more butter than any other region of the country. Indeed, Owatonna proclaimed itself the Butter Capital of the World.

Despite its modest population, Owatonna was served by two railroads and was something of a hub, with 100 retail stores, four hotels and three banks. The National Farmers Bank, housed in an undistinguished red brick building, was presided over by the Bennett family. Carl Bennett, one of the founder's two sons who ran the bank from day to day, was a Harvard graduate and a man whose vision went beyond the borders of small-town Minnesota. When the need for a new bank building became apparent to Bennett, he looked through architectural magazines hoping "to find some architect whose aim it was to express the thought or use underlying a building, adequately, without fear of precedent – like a virtuoso shaping his material into new forms of use and beauty," as he later wrote. The man he found, in 1907, was Louis Sullivan.

If Bennett wanted a bank unlike any other, he had chosen the right man. Sullivan wanted nothing to do with columns, pediments or any of the other Greek temple clichés that announce that you are about enter a place where money is worshipped. With George Elmslie, still on his staff at that time, he created a work of art that has sometimes been described as an ornamented strong box but is more accurately a jeweled box – not a treasury but itself the treasure. Walls, moldings, doors, windows, signs, furniture, tellers' wicket, light fixtures – everything was ornamented. Windows were stained glass, and the light indoors changed throughout the day from season to season. Each detail was not just uniquely designed, but also attentive to the whole. Even the light fixtures alluded to the shape and exterior design of the bank itself. The murals, with their homely rural themes, were not only appropriate to the character of the town and the people who would be doing business in the bank, but celebrated those people and their pursuits.

Although the National Farmers Bank in Owatonna was not Sullivan's last commission, it was his last major architectural statement in the medium of his profession. It is also – as in all his greatest work – a statement that is so individual that it is hard to define, let alone classify. To be sure, throughout his life he took extravagant pains to explicate the meaning of his work, but most of his contemporaries found that they could not follow his explanations beyond a certain point, and as time passed, the more he talked and wrote, the less they listened.

Even today not everyone is quite sure what his message was. Some Bauhaus purists have tended to see Sullivan as little more than the apostle of the decoration they so despise, but surely that is too narrow and doctrinaire a basis for judging his work. Sullivan loved ornament, it is true, but it was only a facet of his architecture, never its point. Like all true architects he strove to create original designs for buildings that would be beautiful, would faithfully express their purpose, would harmonize with their surroundings and would uplift the lives of the people who lived or worked in them. In this endeavor he was prepared to use any technical or aesthetic device that came to hand. And in this endeavor he succeeded magnificently.

National Farmers Bank.
Photo: © Balthazar Korab Ltd.

National Farmers Bank.
Photo: © Cervin Robinson

National Farmers Bank, interior
Photo: © Cervin Robinson

*National Farmers Bank, original
teller's wicket.*
Photo: Courtesy of the
Minnesota Historical Society

*National Farmers Bank,
remodeled teller's wicket.*
Photo: Walter Denny

National Farmers Bank, interior detail.
Photo: Walter Denny

Right:
National Farmers Bank, mural.
Photo: Walter Denny

National Farmers Bank,
chandelier.
Photo: Al Ominsky/Minnesota
Historical Society

*National Farmers Bank, facade
detail.*
Photo: Walter Denny

Left:
Merchants National Bank,
entrance.
Photo: Jack Robertson/Grinnell
2000 Foundation

People's Federal Savings & Loan
Association.
Photo: © Balthazar Korab Ltd.

People's Federal Savings & Loan Association.
Photo: © Balthazar Korab Ltd.

Merchants National Bank, interior.
Photo: © Cervin Robinson

Louis Sullivan
*Farmers & Merchants Union
Bank, 1919, Columbus, WI.*
Photo: Courtesy of Farmers &
Merchants Union Bank

*Farmers & Merchants Union
Bank, stained glass windows.*
Photo: Shorty Seabourne/
Courtesy of Farmers &
Merchants Union Bank

Right:
*Merchants National Bank,
interior, stained glass window.*
Photo: Courtesy of the
Southern Illinois University
Museum

INDEX

PICTURE CREDITS